The Race

ERIC PATTERSON

ISBN 978-0-578-32462-3

ABOUT CROSS COUNTRY RACING

Cross country races are distance running events contested outdoors in all likes of weather. They take place on courses offering varied terrain, uneven footing, and often steep uphills and downhills.

Cross country races attract teams of runners training under the guidance of coaches, but ultimately they are contested by individuals. As you approach the starting line, you pause, contemplating the glory – or disappointment – that might come.

THE RACE

THE RACE

"Do you not know that in a race all the runners run, but only one receives the prize? So run that you may obtain it."

1 Corinthians 9:24

English Standard Version (ESV)

".... Racing and hunting madden the mind.
Precious things lead one astray.
Therefore the sage is guided by what he feels and not by what he sees.
He lets go of that and chooses this."

Tao Te Ching, Chapter 12

Translation by Gia-fu Feng & Jane English

"Some people create with words or with music or with a brush and paints. I like to make something beautiful when I run. I like to make people stop and say, 'I've never seen anyone run like that before.' It's more than just a race.... It's being creative."

Steve Prefontaine

American distance competitor

mid-forties, I was fortunate to be welcomed into a community of passionate runners. With their support, I became re-engaged and reborn as a competitive masters runner. I understood again what it meant to race. And finally the form to this book revealed itself during relaxed moments.

With this small, non-traditional novel (almost a meditation), I have evoked experiences you can inhabit and carry into your life travails, whether artist or athlete, scientist or engineer, creator, helper, or leader. If you are already engaged in what you do, I hope this book affirms and fortifies you. If you have become lost, as I did and still do, I hope this book encourages you and helps you return home.

What are my qualifications to write this book? I asked myself that often during this process. I am a runner. I feel that is enough.

Care to join me on this journey? Let the race begin.

PREFACE

I was a strong student in high school. I worked diligently at my classwork, exams, and assignments. Yet for the foundation that academics built for my college education and future career, I nevertheless felt that the true lessons of school came at cross country practice and races. The important things to learn lied not within the walls of the classroom but in the openness of the cross country course.

How wise we can be when we are young. As an adult, I became a sporadic runner. Yet I remained convinced that cross country racing held mystery that I must comprehend and share. For many years I struggled to bring this book to life. Then near my

EPIPHANY

THE RACE

A lasting story is told not in words but in moments.

At this moment of the race, you run with intention. You stand tall. You sense yourself center. With each breath, with each footstep you act with courage. You answer, "Yes," to the call of the race. You choose to engage.

With that, you relax. Though competing strongly, you feel you do not race hard at all. Your breaths flow in and out, in rhythm with your footsteps, 1-2. You feel open. Energy passes freely. Your strides unfold fluidly.

Your desire for a certain result drives you. A finishing place, a finishing time: Yes, they matter. Yet what you can hold feels less important than what you can experience: the connection to what lies outside you, to all that forms the race.

The earth shifts beneath your feet. You track the course through all its contours.

Other runners engage you: those who press you from behind, those you seek to overtake. You thank them all. They elevate your performance. For them you race your best.

Your teammates pace elsewhere on the course. You feel their presence. Together you prepared for the race. For them you honor your responsibility as a team member. You won't let them down.

Your coach guides you from afar, even as you race into the unknown. You carry advice and assurance as you assess and react to what fate presents you. You feel confident.

Spectators spur you along. To them you offer inspiration. You race with heart.

You are both hero and creator of the story that holds this glorious moment. You are both actor and the conduit through which the story flows.

You are ecstatic.

Then the moment passes. The race continues.

The race ends. The course is dissembled. The other racers depart, as do the spectators. And now you leave the mountain to return to the valley of the everyday.

Your heart holds the remnants of the moment. As long as the moment persists, you sense the courage and determination you applied. You feel the creation and aliveness that coursed through you.

The memory of the moment guides you through the day's distractions. It lends meaning to the pain and drudgery of making it through. It reminds you of what you have been and what you can be.

Alas, the moment finally dims. Always available, but part of a story that has already been told.

How can you know the moment again and experience its glory? How can you bring the moment alive once more to those who bear witness?

You must return to the trial of the race.

That is your Sisyphean curse. One race ends. Another race arrives to prepare for. It does not end.

The thought of the next race consumes you. Life's other obligations seem mundane. Everything is about returning to race, as silly as it might seem to others and even yourself.

Your desire to know the moment drives your training. You wish to be prepared, so you can receive the race's divine secrets and insights.

You are led to a next starting line, one you must cross with full heart.

Do you dare?

ENCOUNTERING THE LINE

THE RACE

As you gaze into the unknown lying beyond the starting line, you feel anxious. Oddly, you welcome this.

For all of the agony that anxiety lays upon you, its presence means the race matters. Something is at stake.

An uncertain journey awaits once you cross the line. The journey holds a promise: of knowing the moment, of revealing who you are. You: glorious, limitless you.

To know you, you must lose you. To engage in the race, you must shed the persona you display within the everyday world. Here in the race you are stripped to your essence: one being among beings, competing for the prize.

In pursuing your goal, you are reduced to your core function: taking in air and pumping oxygen to your tiring muscles. By joining in the chase, you are given to base pain: heavy breathing, pounding heart, burning sinew, sweat, and nausea.

What a steep sacrifice of yourself the race demands, with no guarantee of success.

Yet only by this path will the moment arrive. You

must direct your being in full, without hesitation, towards seizing what you desire: a finishing time or place.

How separate you feel from the glory you wish to know. How conscious you are of what you lack. Competing for your goal will require extraordinary effort from your ordinary self.

You glance at the runners joining you at the starting line. They appear brave, well-prepared, receptive to what is to come. What makes you feel equally deserving of the prize? All of these other runners with great talent and capacity for training. What makes you believe you are qualified?

You too are worthy, you utter. Yes, you belong here. Convince yourself.

Doubts rush to mind. What if you sacrifice yourself, only to fall far short of the result you desire? All of that work and preparation, all for naught.

What if in the midst of the race, inspiration doesn't come? What if you forget how to engage? What if you drift off? There you would flounder, humiliated before the spectators.

Yet – What if you achieve greatness? What if you

know glory?

A strong performance would create expectations that you could repeat it. You would have a duty to succeed, an obligation to be great.

Success could be more hazardous than failure. How you lived before – no more.

How comforting it must be to be ordinary, to not agonize over the conflict between passion and fear. You don't need to encounter the line. You can live a decent life without experiencing the moment. While you stand here alone, others lounge in their homes or among friends. They don't seem to lack.

Many, in fact, pity you. Who would sweat and strain for a prize that concerns so few? Certainly not them! The whole endeavor feels heavy and serious and not much fun. Far more enjoyable to experience sensory excitement: food, drink, music, shows, games. What need for anything more?

You disagree. The race matters.

It matters to the injured, broken runners who are absent. While you come to the line healthy and receptive, these would-be competitors can only watch from the sidelines, outside the borders of the course.

With too much stress, bones can break, muscles tear, wills burn out. The wax on one's wings can melt when flying too close to the sun.

The race also matters to a sad lot of people who, like you, wish to know themselves. Yet they cannot move. They are fully aware of the line. They study it. They walk about it. They have the talent, ability, and aptitude to venture into the race. Yet they lack the will to cross the line. They live in that frustrating place of desire without doing. They wait and long.

You toe the line. You study your teammates who stand shoulder to shoulder with you. Do they feel the same anxiety? Do they question themselves like you do?

You hide – perhaps poorly – the unease that belies.

The line demands that you answer this question: "Do you choose to engage?"

Do you? Do you choose to engage with courage and passion? To willingly sacrifice yourself? To charge into the unknown?

Or do you choose to shirk? To merely make it through?

Fear overwhelms you in this race.

You are afraid to go to that strange, dark place – rife with uncertainty, fraught with pain and sacrifice. You need control! You need security.

So you focus on the result rather than the experience itself. If only the prize could be granted to you without requiring that you engage in the race. You imagine yourself crossing the starting line then crossing the finish line with your desired time and place.

You seek the result because you can cling to it. You wish to grasp that time and place in the midst of your inner turbulence of anxiety. You need to secure the outcome, to drive your destiny.

The more you think of control, the more you press, and the tenser you become. Your legs feel tired, as if blood struggles to flow to them. Your arms feel limited in motion, as if restrained by some bond. Your lungs push against a dense wall and cannot fully expand. All of this constrains rather than enables your ability to perform.

"You need to relax! You need to relax!" you tell yourself. Yet this only makes you tighten more.

In the middle of the race you feel thrust in, rather than someone who arrived willingly. Why are you here? You are a confused visitor.

The race progresses without you, as much as you wish to control the outcome. Clenched yet unengaged, you are closed to the unfolding of your story, to the moment that might arrive.

You do not connect with the other competing runners. They move past, one yard, five yards away, then they are gone. You do not challenge them. You do not race. Only duty carries you towards the finish.

You hope something will change. You hope the gods will breathe inspiration through you. Sadly, you have not sacrificed sufficiently for that to happen, though you feel tired.

Yes, you feel secure, but it is bound to mediocrity. You know who you are and what you are doing, which is merely to go through the motions of racing. Whatever result you get, you get. You feel little different than those who did not face the line.

Go! Go! Pick it up! Stay in touch! You are distressed yet locked into this tale of failure. You give into the way of things to fall apart.

Your performance fails to charge the spectators. Some sense your struggle, but all turn their attention quickly to the other runners who compete in earnest.

Not only do you suffer from your lack of engagement. It takes longer to run the race.

The finish line coasts by at last. You do not seize it. You do not apply some grand flourish to a master work. Instead, your run just... ends. This interminable thing – you cannot call it a race – is through.

Other runners mill about. Chattering excitedly, they tell stories of the race. The pace tested, the competitors engaged, the challenging terrain and weather encountered. You have not taken part. You feel even more remote now than during the race.

You are gracious. You do not diminish the other runners' joy with your sadness. Yet they know: You let them down. You did not contribute to your team. You did not push your competitors.

You know: You let yourself down. The greatest disappointment isn't the lack of result. It is the absence of heart. It is the stunted experience.

The tale of your race is a rambling narrative

lacking creative force. Timidly told with no arc, it simply trails off at the end.

The story has no hero. Facing the line, you chose to be a coward.

When you fail at the race, your spirit is unsatisfied. You retell the tale, quickly reach its insignificant end, then start over, hoping futilely that something will happen. Nothing does.

You desire to advance to the next race, to realize another opportunity to tell a deep, rich story. Until then, your spirit will not keep quiet.

You must prepare.

PREPARATION

THE RACE

You were born to race. You were meant to know glory.

You reflect on how you became drawn to racing. There was a time you did not know the race existed. You discovered racing accidentally as you engaged in an unrelated pastime. Yet though the invitation to race came by chance, it arrived at the right time. You were open to accept. Had the call come any other time, it would not have gone heard.

So you began to race, clumsily. You struggled as you learned this new language of pace – the manner in which you engaged with the race. Sometimes you started off too quickly, then lacked the energy and drive to remain strong to the finish. Sometimes you intentionally plodded along at the beginning, only to discover you had too much ground to make up, even at pell-mell speed. Other times you lost concentration in the middle of the race and simply drifted off in unawareness.

Throughout this frustration with pace and as you strove to become more fit, your race competitors felt far away. They appeared accomplished. Experienced. Sure of their footing, relaxed and fluid. You could not match these other runners, no matter how much you tried to engage them. You always fell short, sometimes at the beginning, sometimes the middle, sometimes the end of the race.

But though you saw little progress, you remained faithful. You practiced hard and exerted yourself in races. For though it might not be expressing itself in finishing times and places, something was shifting inside. You could feel it: your fitness improving, your body and mind aligning with the story waiting to be told.

Then: a breakthrough. Success came not steadily but in breakthroughs. At last, a race came where you felt engaged, where you finally gained a glimpse of understanding. You felt flow. In that race, your performance leapt. You now handled a pace that before had felt impossible. You ran down a rival who had previously seemed unbeatable. You were a runner.

Now the race was joy. You encountered the line with no expectations, no weight, no seriousness. No pause. After the starting gun sounded, you submitted yourself freely to sacrifice. The race was painful, but the novel sensations were pure. You willed yourself through exhaustion and engaged with your competitors. You felt success after you finished a race and held your result. It was easy to dedicate yourself because you were always confident that strong performance would come.

But then you became more aware: Another level of mastery lied above you. You needed to be more serious about practice in order to become faster. You needed to return to the race with higher consciousness so you could accomplish greater things and experience aliveness even more fully.

As you pursued these new goals, defeat began to sting again. As you failed and failed again, you felt hopelessly amateur. You became disheartened. Why did you press at this? How could you believe you would succeed?

Yet amidst such despair, events occurred that felt too appropriate to be coincidence. An unrelated book or article offered insight. A long-lost acquaintance provided encouragement. In unexpected places at unexpected times, the unexpected happened.

Then at last, another breakthrough. And in this

race, you experienced the moment: that power of creativity, that knowledge of greater self.

With that, you greeted and embraced a new person. You had become transformed through preparation and perseverance.

To know that moment: That is why you return to race.

To know that new person: That is why you train.

Except now, it has truly become work. Further mastery will be difficult. Developing into a worthy competitor now seems to have been relatively easy.

You are still ambitious but motivated differently now. Not by the rush of ascension but by the pride of staying. Not by the focus on improvement but by dedication to refinement. Patience, patience and perhaps – perhaps – you will make another breakthrough. In the meantime, you will be a reliable, accomplished teammate.

You have reached a high level of competition with serious stakes demanding a serious work ethic. You approach your workouts and races with an appropriate attitude. This is still play, though. You carry some of your initial romance for the race –

though those early days of innocence, of coming to know the race, will never return.

Success in the race comes not from the gods throwing open the gate by their own accord, welcoming you freely to the glory waiting inside.

Rather, it comes from your consistent discipline: a repeated knocking on that gate – with no assurance it will ever open – until it yields crack by begrudging crack.

Those who dabble in the race – particularly those with talent – might believe the gate will open without requiring the toll of applied, hard work. But in their hearts these runners are being untruthful. They know it. And their lies will be fully exposed by the intensity of the race.

You stand better poised to pass through the gates by simply showing up to practice.

In committing to work you accept the risks. Your sacrifice might be in vain. You might not attain the race results you desire. Luck and circumstance might not work in your favor, or you may simply have sized yourself up wrong: you may in fact be ill-suited for triumph.

With no certainty of payoff, you work for the sake of working. Racing and training are what you do. You attend to all of their details: technique, exertion, diet, rest.

Practice holds no glamour, only humbling penance.

You are one teammate of many under the guidance of your coach. You share a goal calling upon each of you to perform at your best. One key failure or two among you and the cause will be lost. The rewards to the team depend on how greatly you show up as an individual.

As you and your teammates train, you elevate each other. You run in groups that welcome all and abandon none. You joke to lighten your spirits amidst the heaviness. You encourage and check in with each other – particularly your least members – to make sure no one is breaking down.

Most importantly, you demand that each teammate devote their utmost focus and dedication. You all cherish the prize too greatly to tolerate any individual who chooses not to contribute.

You must apply yourself in practice and test yourself in races to have the continued support and companionship of your teammates. They put in the hard work. You must do the same. You cheat your teammates – and yourself – by placing forward anything less.

You had to earn your way into this group. At first some of your teammates acted aloof and cautious. They had met many like you who had entered their house full of talk and enthusiasm, only to depart quickly when they discovered the cost of becoming a resident. Other teammates were guarded, viewing you as a trespasser intent on seizing the territory they had worked so hard to secure.

Still other teammates were generous, however. They understood they inhabited a special place and wished to share its treasures. These teammates were patient and friendly, hoping you would develop as a runner, for you might be key to the team achieving its goal. In any case, they were wiser to embrace you rather than fear you, for it was through your prodding that they would sharpen their own performances.

What an exciting culture to which these teammates invited you, dedicated to the race! This way of life has its outer trappings: clothing, shoes, and battle dress in which you adorn yourself. Racing too has characteristic food, music, and humor.

Racing also has its own language, which you seek to comprehend and express yourself in. You immerse yourself in racing's literature to fill yourself with knowledge and soak in inspiration. You listen to lore for the heartbeat of the race.

But most importantly, racing has its community. As runners you share a common knowing. Outsiders might not understand your motives to race and what you hope to gain. You do. They might not sense the details you notice during the race. You do.

Outsiders might not appreciate the hard work a runner invests before performing on race day. You do.

You walk through the gates and step onto the track.

You scan its oval circuit, precisely measured to 400 meters. You note the painted lanes, evenly spaced.

No one else has arrived.

You jog slowly, warming up in the track's outermost lane. You focus on the day's planned workout and what you intend to accomplish. The trial will take place over there, in the reserved inside lane.

Time and distance might dissolve during the moments of the race, but they are central to proper training. To deem the workout a success, you must run precise distances at precise times appropriate for you: no slower, no faster.

The workout has a specific purpose, whether of easy, moderate, or hard intensity, sprint or long distance, brief or full rest between intervals. It addresses a specific component of fitness and requires it be completed the right way.

A successful workout calls for effort, certainly. To become stronger in body and mind, you must tax yourself. You must sweat, concentrate, and suffer to achieve your goal times. You must overcome the resistance to do the work.

Yet pride yourself too much on working harder than other runners – place greater effort into each workout than warranted – and you will tear yourself down without giving yourself opportunity to recover. You might celebrate yourself as a champion of workouts yet have too little strength or energy for the race itself.

You ready yourself for the workout by reciting your target times and the intermediate split times leading to them. Nothing less, nothing more this day.

Your teammates join you now on this jog. Your coach walks onto the track, stopwatch in hand.

Hard work ahead.

"Listen carefully to me. Do as I say," your coach says. "But don't be afraid to speak up."

In designing the program – the grand plan to guide you – your coach starts at the end: targeting the race where your team will succeed (the race witnessed by the most spectators), then choosing the workouts, intermediate races, and sequence that will progress you towards that final test. In order to achieve your coveted times and places – and to realize your glory in those pursuits – you trust in your coach's wisdom and experience.

You place faith in your coach, who presents a path, a way to knowing. You fully embrace your coach's word, for it has led many previous runners to the space you desire to inhabit.

To confirm you follow that right path, you attend to data. You examine your workout times and study your past race results. Yet you also heed intuition. And when in doubt, you approach your coach for assurance.

But when something doesn't feel right to your training, you are wise to let your coach know. If a workout doesn't achieve what is intended or if you have a lackluster race tied to your preparation, your coach and you need to make a change. Staying true to the overall training philosophy, you alter the program: substitute a new workout for the old, train with greater intensity or less, refine technique, alter diet.

This is good. The ability to adapt is the sign of a healthy system and a healthy coach. Your training is a process of evolution. It demonstrates how successfully you and your coach have partnered. The greatest expression of your preparation will come during the final test.

"Time to work," your coach says.

You would continue to avoid the mark if it were up to you. Your teammates feel the same. You have moved slowly to arrive here: dressing lazily, jogging slowly to engage your muscles, stretching quietly as a group. You wait now for your coach's direction.

This trial has weight. Throughout the week you have anticipated this workout. You have focused on it today as you struggled to concentrate on life's other matters.

Your coach offers simple, direct instructions. You will run this number of intervals, at these distances, with these durations of rest. Run in these particular, short amounts of time.

These short amounts of time. That is what you attend to.

The workout presses you beyond the light taxations of everyday. It challenges you to approach the intensity of the race. But you must hold yourself just short. You must leave something for the race. You must remain fresh, energetic, and driven.

Align yourself with a peak. Venture into the rugged mountains. Then wait patiently before summiting.

The workout calls for you to sacrifice without immediate, explicit reward. Such an arduous task few will witness, requiring you trust in its future benefits. During the workout you will suffer many of the same pains of the race without experiencing its glory. You can only imagine great results coming at some time, maybe. No wonder so many hesitate to take it on. They choose comfort instead.

While others laugh and relax in the warm indoors with friends, you and your teammates perform in an open, non-ornate venue for an audience of one: a coach who is here not to appreciate but to critique.

"It don't happen without doing. Let's go."

You step to the mark. A group of teammates join you, two per row in several rows. You study the ground, then raise your head to peer at the empty lane of track ahead.

"Hit it," your coach says, simultaneously starting a stopwatch.

The first steps of the workout are hardest. You draw your legs forward, disbelieving you are committed. Immediately you begin counting how much interval work you have completed and how much remains to be done.

After those disjointed first steps, you settle with your teammates into what feels an appropriate pace. Yet it is difficult to gauge what effort results in what split time, no matter how many workouts you have experienced. So much to take into account: your energy levels, the weather, the track condition, the boost that comes at the start of work, and so forth.

You pass through the first checkpoint, upright and heads forward. "Too fast!" your coach calls sharply, followed by how many seconds you are ahead of schedule.

You adjust and slow down. At the next split, you step past the coach on time. This pace, if held steady, will ensure you hit your target time.

You breathe heavily now and sigh occasionally from the toil. Already your legs have become tired and unresponsive. Yes, this is work.

You struggle to concentrate. The novelty of the start is long gone. The track's mundaneness is apparent. Your mind wanders from the task at hand.

Focus!

You train upon your goal time. It presents itself as a jutted rock for which to grasp. Exhausted, you consider not reaching for it, to instead hold steady just below.

You sustain your pace, remaining in step with your teammates. You all have made a pact. You will achieve this time. Someone at times will grunt a few words of encouragement or discipline through an outbreath. More often, the impetus to press on comes wordlessly. Someone within the group – sometimes you – surges when others flag.

Your teammates and you do not compete. You cooperate. You are practicing, not racing. You seek to ready all runners in your group, not just a few. For your team to succeed in the race, you must all succeed in this workout.

The interval's completion draws close. Ahead stands your coach, holding the watch. To this point you have held the pace required to hit the goal time. You must keep up with your teammates and maintain your drive to the end, despite your exhaustion.

The distance to the mark grows shorter. Then you are through.

Your coach calls out the final time with a neutral voice. On target. Good. This one done well. You need to hit the rest of the times, though.

Your teammates and you have little time to reflect. You rest only long enough to recover your breath. Soon comes the next interval, another goal time to meet. And soon after the next interval starts, you are tired and in pain.

So the intervals repeat, with exact, attended precision, with exact, attended regularity.

The middle intervals are difficult. You are weary and by your count have much work left to do. Your teammates and you continue to provide each other resolve.

Your coach oversees your group's quality of effort, asking occasionally that you check your heartbeats, assigning a few extra seconds of rest if needed.

At the start of the final interval, you feel a little lighter. The overall goal of the workout feels attainable. You need only maintain. Through this last interval's middle stretches, you summon a source of strength other than your teammates. You conjure the spirits of champions past and present. How did they perform on these trying occasions, when no one else was watching? Can you run with the same heart?

You burst through the finish for the last time. When your coach calls out your successful time, you punch the air.

You bend over and breathe heavily. You give a teammate a low hand slap. Now you can fully recover.

You hear the same quiet that has been present since the start. No cheers or applause today. The only prizes you garner are those you bestow upon yourself. The satisfaction of this workout done well. The tastiness of this drink of water.

The time to race has drawn near.

"I can offer nothing more," your coach says. "It is now upon you."

To this point you have depended on your coach. You have trusted in your coach's choices, instruction, and guidance. Your coach has assured you of how aptly you have worked out, and of how strongly you have performed in the races leading to this next one.

Now you are alone. Yet you feel confident: healthy and well-conditioned. You have practiced with quiet diligence and dedication. You have done the work.

Your preparation has built a foundation. It has also aligned you with the task that lies ahead. You are in position. You are receptive now to inspiration. A favorable outcome feels possible.

Performance differs altogether from practice, however. Performance requires audacity. Performance calls for you to be both brave and foolhardy.

With practice, you gather wood. With performance, you set it ablaze. First you need a spark.

Prepared. Yes, you are. Now to venture to the race.

THE RACE

THE RACE

THE RACE

The cross country course appears arbitrary when you and your teammates first encounter it. Without cones and barriers placed as markers, this area holds a different purpose. Today it provides a site where you will test yourself. The course makers have devised this: every boundary, straightaway, turn, uphill, downhill. Every smooth swath of grass, every patch of gravel or mud. Every challenge and every chance to regroup.

You walk the course to become familiar, but you won't really know it until you engage.

The race is bound by its rules, both written and unspoken. But outside those agreements lie no limits to what you can experience. It's expressed in the openness around you: the miles of trail ahead, the expanse of sky above.

Here rests a void. You, as a runner, will breathe into it. You will inspire.

The course is a stage, a sacred space. The spectators respect this. They remain outside its boundaries. If they must cross, they scamper, as if to leave no trace of their footsteps.

You set off on a warm-up jog with your

teammates along the course, your loose-fitting sweats serving as curtains to your racing uniforms. You are about to perform. The spectators gaze at you; you are aware of them. You sense both their longing and their pity. They desire some gift from you but apologize for how you will need to suffer.

You attend instead to your teammates. As you warm up, you accustom your minds and muscles to the struggle that lies ahead. You anticipate what might come on this very ground. You tune your strides to the rhythm of the upcoming race.

What a spectacle! Other runners share the course, the colors and logos on their team uniforms announcing them as competitors. You intermingle and pass by each other. No one ventures far from the starting line, however. The line maintains its hold.

Everything is about the line. The runners know this. Just as the course makers have dictated the path and terrain along which you will compete, so too have they drawn the line. These disparate teams and personalities coming from disparate places: the line is where you will converge.

You feel anxious again as you approach the line and consider the uncertainty on the other side. You understand the distance from the glory you hope to know. You acknowledge the sacrifice and patience its pursuit will entail. Nevertheless, your mind threatens to panic. The desire for the result, the clinging to security and control, the doubt of your worthiness: all threaten to undermine your performance and keep you in the world of the ordinary.

You breathe deeply and feel your feet on the ground. Proof of glory is the wrong thing to chase. The experience of glory: that will transform you and remain with you. The finishing time and place – if they are to be – are mere artifacts.

As much as you wish to secure the result, control is impossible. The race will unfold as it will. It will depend on rain or sleet, heat or cold. It will depend not only on your condition and performance but on those of your competitors. And you can know no certainty when so much is left to chance: multiple runners in close quarters, unpredictable surges in the pace, sudden changes in the course's terrain.

You will test yourself to see how large you can

become. But you can accept only what your body will give you, only what the race will present. To that you surrender. To know glory, you are invited to let go of attachment to the outcome of the race.

So many runners with greater mastery than you. Yet as plain as you feel: Yes, you are qualified to share the line. You can only be yourself, replete with gaps and limitations. Forgive yourself your shortcomings. You are enough.

You relax. You release to the flow of things. You feel yourself open. You welcome the gods to help you.

You descend into the crucible of the race. Images of past races and remnants of past moments come to you. They move you. You step into the story you are about to tell, the story you will live.

As you gaze beyond the line, your coach comes before you.

"Do you want to know the secret to peak performance?"

"Sure," you reply.

"I'd tell you," your coach says, "but then there'd be no sport to it."

THE RACE

You smile softly. You step across the line and stride your final warm-up. You feel the rhythm, the familiarity of your motions. With each footstep down the course, the tether of the line grows weaker.

You are alert. You are ready to be surprised by what is to come and just as ready to respond.

You return to the line. To know yourself, you will need to lose yourself. Yes, you feel confident from the hours of preparation and hard work. Yet the quality of your performance hinges on how you answer the key question.

Do you choose to engage?

Yes, you choose to engage.

It is time to race.

"Runners, to the line!"

So you all step forward, a kaleidoscope of clothing colors representing the scattered places from where you have arrived.

You glance at your teammates next to you. To this moment, you have chattered. Joked. Nervously laughed. Now you are quiet.

You study the line at your feet. Something is at stake. You breathe in deeply, let it leave slowly. Ah. There will be many breaths, many steps before this race is through.

Far beyond this line is a finish you can sense but cannot see. Out there in the green expanse you will create an experience. You will tell a story. Its truth will depend on your courage and presence.

"Runners, take your mark."

You arrive feeling so lonely, so separate from what lies out there. You want to know it. You want to know yourself. You want to come home.

All you can know right now is this still point. Hope lies in your openness to what the race presents. Faith will be applied each footstep after willful footstep.

You look at the starter now, one arm stretched to hold the runners back. The other arm is pointed skyward, holding the pistol whose crack will send you forward into the unknown.

"Runners, set..."

Then you are off. With that, your anxiety vanishes. You no longer fear the unknown. You are in the unknown. You are committed to the race. There is no escape now, not without humiliation. You will see this test through to the finish.

Every story has a beginning, middle, and end. And every story receives its impetus from its center, from its performer.

You will tell your story. Performing for an audience of spectators, inspired by the gods, you will share your rich experience. Race with a pace, rhythm, and tempo in sync with the way of things, and your story will flow. Weave your story with those of the other runners, and the story of the race will be told.

On the other hand, work counter to what is meant to be – or don't engage at all – and you will present a disappointing tale – or a bore.

At the start of the race, all things are possible.
Everything is poised to take form here in the open.

Past the starting line, the spectators line the path, forming a channel through which you all stream. They cheer. They call their heroes forward.

You press ahead at your initial pace. You start to perform. You begin to create.

Other runners charge away from you, propelled by the excitement of the start. Some are more accomplished; you will not see them again until the finish. Others have unknowingly been swept forward by the rush.

You feel you are running too slowly, as if you are wading into the race. It's okay. Find your center. Divorce yourself from the other runners for now. Focus on your race.

Stand tall. Breathe. Have patience. Be confident. The runners with unsteady grounding will return to you.

You relax. You open to the unfolding of the race.

Everyday life is disjointed. Everyone wants something from you. Everything around you calls out to delight or distract.

THE RACE

Here in the race, you attend to the essential: the rhythm, the counting of your breaths and footsteps.

In this moment, you lose sense of time.

In the race's middle stage, it is the quiet that challenges you the most. Lacking the charge of the race's start or the pull of its finish, the middle of the race presents only dull miles. It seems to merely connect the race's far more dramatic parts. Surely, the spectators feel this way. Most throng near the race's start and finish lines, while relatively few provide support here.

You feel anonymous for the length of these middle miles. Here you are, just another runner. The middle tests your character. When no one else is watching, how do you choose to perform?

The middle stage is not glamorous. It does not invite clamor. The middle miles do not pass quickly or easily. They are work.

Regardless you must approach these miles with a fresh mind and vigorous pace. If you lose focus and concentration here, the energy and momentum that propelled you at the race's start will simply peter out. And if they disappear now, there's little hope they will revive for the race's completion.

The spectators might not celebrate the work of the middle, but it matters. It matters. You runners wage the race here in the seeming nothingness of the middle.

You thank your teammates who join you in this journey. You praise the competitors who press you in this exercise.

Yet ultimately, you face these middle miles alone. The race demands you be present – without the help of a crowd.

You cannot control many of the circumstances that shape the race. You concede that. Yet you can claim responsibility for your pace, the impetus you apply to racing.

You must find the right pace that places you fully in the race and can be sustained to the finish. Press too hard – force the breaths too far before the footsteps – and you will tire too soon and trail off rapidly. Press too lightly – let the footsteps lag too far behind the breaths – and you will not perform to your capability.

To know the appropriate pace, you must listen. You must be receptive to what the race presents. You put forward a pace but adjust it to the paces of your competitors. You notice whether the terrain and weather are helping or hindering you.

You approach the race not with a set of steps to follow but with a general idea of how you propose to engage. You will readily revise your strategy, however, based on how the mystery of the race reveals itself.

The story of your race will turn based on resolute decisions you make at unforeseen times. As you race, you are present and alert, prepared to respond when those times arrive.

You trust yourself. You trust in the way of things. You can paddle the canoe, but the river's current determines how fast you might go.

You are grateful for your competitors. You are connected. In fact, you cooperate. Your competitors help you stay focused and involved in the race by fully engaging you. They challenge you to attain that right pace where you know your power. Likewise, you owe it to your competitors to invest your heart in the race. To not test them would be an affront.

You contest every runner for place. You resolve to remain ahead of the runners behind. You strive to retain contact with the runners up front. You engage your competitors with each foot strike.

You do not give up. You compete no matter how small or futile the act may seem. No matter whether any spectator pays attention.

The breaths of life flow down the back of your throat, welcomed by your lungs that expand like a bellows. Oxygen feeds the fire that energizes your pace. Smiling, you exhale and propel forward, your stride lengthening, your arms pulling through, the terrain moving beneath your feet.

Stepping in time, you run open and relaxed. You pace upright, a straight line passing from the heavens through you to the earth. You are not merely a performer. You are a conduit for a creative force, manifesting itself in the story you tell. You feel this power flow through you with no resistance.

You race. You are thankful. You are alive.

You are not the first to race here. This course has history. Through the grass and between the trees, you pace a well-worn path. Others before you faced similar trials. Many raced with courage and knew their greatness. Some of their names are familiar, but most are lost to time. Yet all of their footsteps are part of the course's texture. Their stories – and the larger stories of their races – are imbued in the course's lore and mystique.

You race in these runners' legacies and create your own.

The course brings its flourishes. It rolls. It contracts. It invites. It hinders.

No two race courses are alike. Each presents itself in its own manner. One might contain hills long and steep, another flat stretches of hardscrabble, yet another narrow paths with sharp bends. Another might present a combination of all three.

Course conditions may vary, as may the weather. After all, the race is held outdoors, in the open air. It may be staged on hard ground, soggy underfooting, mud, or snow. It may occur in rain, cold, or blazing sun.

You shape the quality of your experience not only by how strongly you engage your competitors but by how bravely you face the terrain and elements. Some course aspects and weather conditions you take on with confidence, others with dread. You account for your strengths and weaknesses.

The course underlies a greater collective experience. As personally as you encounter it, the course is common to all. The same course tests all race competitors equally, no matter how greatly you differ in talent, experience, and achievement.

THE RACE

The course is the space where the stories take place.

Staying present, you connect to the race at a fundamental level: through your breaths and footsteps.

First, your breaths. In, out. In, out. In: your lungs expand with the oxygen needed to drive your limbs. Out: your lungs expel the carbon dioxide from your spent muscles. In: like a swing pulling back to a suspended position that can be held no longer, then out: pushing forth to become suspended at another furthest point. In, you take in what the race presents; out, you drive yourself into its midst.

With each in-breath and out-breath you feel destruction and creation in their purest states.

With each in-breath, you are dying. You are one breath closer to your last, when you will return to earth. You gasp for another breath of life to sustain you in the race. For outside this state of destruction, separate from the pain and suffering that seek your surrender, you sense greatness.

With each out-breath, you feel forceful. You create a story of courage as you propel yourself towards that glorious moment of knowing. You make bold strikes against the nature of things to fall apart. With your out-breaths you smile. In the presence of the gods you share your experience of aliveness with the spectators.

Now, your footsteps. With each in-breath, you count 1, 2 footsteps, then with each out-breath you count 1, 2. In: 1, 2, out: 1, 2, as you maintain this pace, this tempo, this cadence. On this you meditate.

Every footstep counts. With each footstep, you apply vigor and quality, not for what you can achieve but simply because it is right. It is proper.

Too many people approach their work not caring. Not you. You race for the sake of the race, with no guarantees of glory or reward, fame or compensation. No one beyond this course may know it, but you know it, your competitors know it, and the spectators who witness you know it. The gods know it too.

Each of your footsteps is not only for now but for eternity. The achievement will date, the memory of the race will fade. But the courage you bring to each footstep will ripple beyond the boundaries of this course, across people and planet, across time.

This is integrity. This is truth. This is how best you can say, "Thank you," for this gift of life.

As you race, you experience the race. As you perform, you observe yourself. You feel separate from your ordinary self... you've surpassed it, really. You are the hero of a story that you tell, a story of doubt and bravery, temptation and resolve, decay and determination, exhaustion and elation. This story is being created not only by you but by your competitors, the terrain, and the spectators.

You are but a conduit for this story. You invited it here by preparing, relaxing, and opening yourself. Now, without you needing to do anything but be, the story flows through you, then everywhere, imbued by your quality. You inform the story and make it distinctly yours.

Swept by the story, you become present. You lose sense of time and place. Split times and course landmarks become important not on their own but as confirmation that your story is progressing well.

Your story weaves into the stories of the many other runners to become the story of the race. And the story of the race – and the stories of many other races – contribute to the most profound story of all.

So much depends on how strongly you engage in

the race. On how greatly you tell your story.

You must sacrifice yourself to know yourself: to know your own greatness, to know the largeness you are, to know the glory that transcends the ordinary. You accepted the cost of sacrifice when you answered the call of the race.

The point is not merely to inflict pain upon yourself. It would be masochism – self-torture – to do so without hoping to gain something in return. No, your sacrifice is a negotiation. With open eyes you give yourself up in order to receive the knowing.

The deal requires you constantly pay. Your lungs gasp for air. Your heart pounds to its maximum. Your arms tire, your legs flag as your stored energy is spent. Your body calls for you to cease.

But if you surrender to the pain, if you stop racing or even slow down, then the possibility of knowing will be gone. All you have invested will be lost. All of your preparation will have been for nothing.

Each breath, each footstep, then, is a choice. Do you succumb to the pleas of your body? Do you let yourself be pulled to earth? Do you give in to mediocrity as you have before?

Or do you persist?

Sustaining your pace is the courage you bring to the race.

With mind, body, and spirit, you will yourself forward. You drive on, no matter how uncertain it appears that the moment will come. As you persevere, you venture deeper into the divine.

You continue. You endure. As humbled as you are, you also feel expansive. Stronger forces have come into play. Benevolent gods speak through you. You breathe in and out the stardust of the universe.

For that is the meaning. The race reveals what has always lied within and without you. In the race you come home.

You have let go of your everyday self. Who are you now? Your breaths in and out, your footsteps upon the ground, the terrain before you, your competitors about you, your coach and teammates supporting you, you running tall with your head in the sky. You are larger than when you arrived.

Onward you strive towards your goal: that place, that time. Yet as you feel the actor, you feel acted upon. You sense inspiration moving through you openly. You feel a powerful drive. Energy flows freely. As quickly as you pace, you feel you do not run hard at all.

You tell an unfolding story that has always existed, like the sculpture beneath the marble. The story has come forth – become created – by your choice, because of your willingness to sacrifice. With heart and courage, you perform. You reach beyond you: to the spectators, to the gods.

You have arrived at this place through preparation and resolve, through the knock-knock-knocking of discipline. Now you have come to a knowing, because you have prevailed. You have lasted.

You have touched the divine. From this comes joy. This is a dance, an epiphany.

This is success. You can feel proud and unashamed, for you have performed with integrity, for the encounter has been true.

You have engaged.

You sense the approach of the finish line – a different type of line. The starting line is characterized by openness and anticipation; the finish line is defined by closure.

You desire to finish your race heroically. You have experienced that moment. Now you want to complete the story you have been creating. You wish this story to be great, not merely good. Greatness would come from leaving this course with something you can carry: that on which you have trained, the desired time and place.

To this point you have paced with the finish line in the back of your mind, meting out your energy based on how far you still had to go. Now things feel urgent. The distance to the finish has grown short.

Throughout the intensity of the middle miles, you appeased your body with false assurances that the end of the race was near. Now that it truly is, your body's pain has become excruciating. You wish it to cease. You can scarcely move your legs. Your lungs hurt from their desperate gasps. Your heart strains from its rapid beats.

For the spectators the race has become its most

compelling. The positioning game the runners played quietly during the race's middle stage has set up this final contest. The spectators flock to the stretch of the course before the finish line.

You connect to these spectators witnessing the race from outside the boundaries. As you stand tall on stage, you feed off their energy: their attention, their encouragement, their cheers and applause. Your pain and sacrifice have been for them as well as for your knowing.

A competitor pulls alongside, challenging you. Are you worthy of matching this rival? The finish line lies ahead. You see a clock display, ticking closer to the time you desire to best. You doubt whether you are deserving.

So close to the end. One last critical moment. Will you exert your will to finish strongly? Do you have the heart to carry through?

The race calls for you to make one final sacrifice. If you so choose you can feel no regret, regardless of result. You cannot know how much strength and drive your competitor has remaining. You can only resolve for yourself: When you cross the finish line, all of your energy will have been spent.

You deny your pain. You do not slow down. You pull forward your exhausted legs. You pump your weakening arms. You lean ahead to drive momentum

The finish line is just a few yards away. You are a step ahead of your rival. Your desired finishing time is still within reach.

You did it!

The time and finish. You are surprised! You cannot believe you have achieved this. Sometime in the future, when you look back at this result, you will feel it was achieved by someone else.

The race is over. The pain is through.

You place your hands on your knees to hold yourself up. You struggle to catch your normal breath. Your heartbeat remains high. But you are confident that in time, you will recover.

You shake the hand of your rival. You thank. You praise. This competitor deserves your respect. You glance back towards the finish line and watch other competitors complete their races.

You seek out your teammates. You share your stories. You congratulate each other and what you have accomplished. Yes! Our team has succeeded! Though you encountered your races individually, you made this journey together. Now you have a collective story to take away.

Your coach pats you on the back. "Great race. You'll always have this with you."

The artifacts of this achievement – your place, your time – will date. But that moment of glory you experienced will be timeless. It will always be available – through the story that evokes it.

You will return to the everyday world with the truth you have come to know about yourself in this sacred space. You will be able to call upon it in times of doubt, when you need fortification.

The spectators will leave with their own understanding.

You take a deep breath, let it out slowly. Now is the time to rest and reflect.

THE RACE

RETURNING

THE RACE

THE RACE

You appreciate what you learn from racing and preparation. You apply these insights often in life's races taking place outside the course. You continue to return to the race.

Each trial is but one of many. Each demands courage. Each strengthens resolve. Each reveals truth. Each trial produces a story that becomes part of your greater life story.

Each trial requires preparation. Without it, the experience lacks substance. You prepare whether you are pleased or unhappy with your results, whether you have known glory or not.

When racing seems empty of meaning, you ask yourself, Is this all it is?

Yes, it is.

When you race, you attend to each breath, each footstep. At the same time, you acknowledge the preparation and previous trials that have led you here. You foresee the work and encounters to come. In this sense, present, past, and future exist at once.

To race is to create. To race is to know. To race is to be alive.

The race is all.

THE RACE

ACKNOWLEDGEMENTS

I am grateful to the many individuals who helped me grow and develop as a runner and to those who provided feedback and encouragement on this book.

My younger brother Marc was a high school cross country teammate and my number one fan. He has also been a vociferous booster of the book. My late father was a tremendous writer who taught me at a young age that the key to successful writing was putting in the hard work of rewriting. Thanks to him for his advice on this manuscript. My mother provided high praise when she said she understood now why running was so important to me in high school.

I am thankful for the love, support, and patience of my family over the many years it required for this book to emerge. To my former wife, Donna Wilson Herrmann, thank you. I owe gratitude too to my children Ari, Madelyn, Sarah, Teran, and Aurora.

Thank you to the friends, family members, and running community members who reviewed drafts of the book, including Sam Simkin, Bruce Wilson, Rick Bruess, Laura Bruess, Liz Knapp, Carah Wertheimer, Angela Bevacqua, Karen Laslo Franklin, kylan Marsh, Sandy Brown, and Alex Wilsdon. I deem you all Race participants.

I benefited incredibly from the guidance of my high school cross country coaches Ron Schreiner and Ken Wentzel as I developed from a near dead-last freshman runner to varsity athlete. I also improved from keeping pace with my teammates in practice and in meets. Their humor and camaraderie also made even interval workout days enjoyable. At risk of leaving someone out, I'd like to call out Jack Ashburner, Dave Bruni, Frank Firsching, Nick Fitzgerald, Pete Fleming, Mark Goetz, Jon Kaplan, Bill Kracklauer, Mark Lewis, Will Loftis, Tim McLain,

Jack McMahon, Dave Martinelli, Chris Nabors, Eric Pittore, Tim Regan, Mickey Rihtarchik, Matt Truesdell, Bob Weiner, John Wessels, John Wright, Lisa Thompson, and Debbi Fitzgerald.

I credit my rejuvenation as a runner in my forties to the competitive masters running groups that welcomed me in. These passionate runners showed up to race Saturday morning after Saturday morning, on rugged courses at odd distances in all forms of weather, including eight inches of fresh snow. Thanks to them I understand racing in its purest form, when it truly is about the race. I'd like to express thanks to Tom LeMire, Dave Dooley, Woody Green, Lorraine Green, Don Hayes, Jeff Dumas, Ken Thurow, Marlys Thurow, Mike Engle, Rich Holston, Jerry Greenwald, Doug Brandmier, Jim Reynolds, Verne Carlson, Vicki Hunter, Brian Hunter, Elisabeth Kandel, Dan Fogelberg, Rodger Kram, Chuck Lawrie, Pete Richards, Joyce LeMire, Amie Durden, Benji Durden, Jill Sellars, Steve Sellars, Irving Weiss, Eda Leptich, Deb Conley, David Rothenburger, Scott Kukel, Jeremy Johnson, Keith Johnson, Jennifer Forker, Michael Quispe, Eric Albright, George Forbes,

THE RACE

Brandon Rockwood, Robert Kanieski, David Blankinship, Rick Granquist, John Brackney, and Shaun Schafer. Thanks also to Rich Sandoval, Louise Adams, Claire Benton, Thomas David Kehoe, Jim Gilbert, Adam Haron, Samantha Schwind, and Linda Batlin.

I gained insight for this book as well by being part of vibrant church and oral storytelling communities. I share my appreciation for the spiritual leadership of the Revs. Lowell Uda, Howell Lind, and Kelly Dignan.

Finally, I am grateful for the chance encounters with Tony Mangan, Ted Tucker, and Tom Shellenberg who demonstrated the audacity of following their dreams.

The cover photo is by the Irish Defence Forces of the 2012 Defence Forces Cross Country Championships. It is licensed under the Creative Commons Attribution 2.0 Generic License (https://creativecommons.org/licenses/by/2.0/deed.en).

ABOUT THE AUTHOR

Eric Patterson competed as a scoring member of his high school varsity cross country team in western Pennsylvania. Much later in life, he twice completed the Bolder Boulder 10K in under 40 minutes as a grand masters runner. Eric has worked as a magazine writer and journalist, and has also performed as an oral storyteller at several Colorado festivals. He lives in Boulder, Colo.

THE RACE

Made in the USA
Monee, IL
02 November 2022

16979430R00059